Jesus Crisis

Phiwa Langeni

Do not think that I have come to bring peace to the earth; I have not come to bring peace, but a sword. - Matthew 10:34 (NRSV)

Many a cartoon character has swung a sword haphazardly, their (un)intended targets escaping the consequences that would've befallen them had they encountered a real sword. Sword enthusiasts undoubtedly cringe to see these misrepresentations.

Likewise, Jesus enthusiasts—back then and now—likely cringe at his sharp words. We often imagine a child-inviting, good-news-bringing, body-and-spirit-healing Jesus. Alas, this double-sided Jesus is difficult to witness.

Of all the things he could've brought instead of peace, why bring a sword? My guess? Precision. From the metals utilized to the length, weight, and style, real-life swords are deliberately designed for their specific uses, making cartoon-like gestures nearly impossible without injuring oneself; that is, before the blade does. When used correctly, their slashes are nearly surgical.

With a meticulous commitment to justice, Jesus cuts into our world with a tool of destruction. Unlike typical sword wielders, though, he severs the systems that oppress those most in need. He dissects the divisions that perpetuate violence. He hacks the hate that poisons our shared divinity.

We've become so familiar with our communal sinfulness and individual unwellness that healing feels like a threat. That makes Jesus' unexpected tool choice even more essential because purposeful incisions do less damage than the jagged tears from prolonged stressors.

After a year of one crisis after another, clinging to what we've known is a natural choice. However, in this time of anticipation, might we embrace this new Crisis who arrives in the form of a tiny little baby?

PRAYER

Come, O Long-Awaited Crisis! Be near us, we pray, as we prepare for your arrival with purpose and precision.

A Righteous Branch

Vince Amlin

"The days are surely coming, says God, when I will fulfill the promise I made to the house of Israel and the house of Judah. In those days and at that time I will cause a righteous Branch to spring up for David; and he shall execute justice and righteousness in the land."

- Jeremiah 33:14-15 (NRSV)

Every week in staff meeting, our sexton updates us on the replacement tree the city has promised us for the easement in front of the church. A storm blew through last summer and cracked the old oak in two. A couple weeks later, the Bureau of Forestry finished the job.

The stump showed well over a hundred rings. Then they ground that down too. No hope of a shoot springing up spontaneously.

So our sexton keeps us updated. Every week. And every week the update is: still waiting.

It doesn't matter that it's been over a year with no change. It doesn't matter when I say, "We've got a lot to cover today." It doesn't matter when I get snippy and insist, "I think everyone is aware of the situation!"

He keeps it on the agenda.

Like those who persist in the cause of righteousness and justice. The ones who sound the alarm. The ones who point to what is missing, what has been destroyed.

The ones who won't let it drop. Even though it makes things awkward. Even though people get snippy. Even though there has been no change and everyone is aware of the situation.

Because everyone is aware of the situation and there has been no change.

They keep it on the agenda. Every week. Every day. They hold to the promises that have been made.

PRAYER

Righteous one, keep your promises.

Righteous one,
    keep your promises.

November 29, 2021

Someone Else's Time

Liz Miller

But do not ignore this one fact, beloved, that with the Lord one day is like a thousand years, and a thousand years are like one day. - 2 Peter 3:8 (NRSV)

When the work ahead is daunting—whether it is dismantling white supremacy, reversing climate change, or ridding the world of its many phobias—it soothes us to say, "This is the work of the next generation." We will do what we can, of course, but we don't really expect change until someone else is in a position of power or has better ideas than we have.

We solidify this division of labor with our definition of generations, measuring only in 20- to 30-year increments, doling out responsibilities and assignments accordingly. This generation caused the financial crisis; the next is called to solve it. This generation enacted civil rights; the next moves us past tolerance. No matter the issue at hand, the underlying message is the same: it is someone else's job to fix this mess.

But through God's eyes, where decades pass like seconds and centuries are the same length as sitcoms, the divisions are meaningless. Pointing the finger of blame or kicking the can of justice down the road might make us feel better in the moment, but all God sees is a thousand years of people harming each other. Hasn't God waited long enough? May we not let one more day pass before uniting in our efforts to move from hurt to healing.

PRAYER

Dear God, we promise to work together to clean up this mess, even if it takes a thousand years. Amen.

November 30, 2021

Lift Your Heads, Again

Mary Luti

"Now when these things begin to take place, stand up and raise your heads, because your redemption is drawing near." - Luke 21:28 (NRSV)

A friend told me she finds Advent frustrating. Every year we lift our heads, stand on tiptoe, watch for Christ to bring in the new age, and nothing happens. After 2,000 years, her toes are starting to go numb, her enthusiasm's waning. Advent feels sort of routine.

Scripture says that for God, a thousand years are like a day. By divine standards, we have short attention spans. If Advent feels routine, maybe we have a skewed sense of time. But it could also be that we're harboring the illusion that we're OK. Even amid pandemics and wars and political upheaval, we persist in that delusion. Maybe we get tired of waiting because we don't really need what we're waiting for.

I go through my days with my Visa in one hand and the Golden Rule in the other, and with them I shape a mostly adequate life. And as long as it's not disrupted in some truly disastrous way, I don't feel a crying need to be redeemed. I pray with the church, "Come, Lord Jesus!" But under my breath I'm begging, "Just not right now." As someone once quipped, if you're having a decent year in your own kingdom, it's hard to long sincerely for the coming of God's.

If Advent feels frustrating, or boring, or beside the point, maybe it's because we haven't gotten real enough yet to need what it promises. Or to perceive and care about how much others need it.

One more time, then. Let's prop up our heads and keep them lifted again, this year and year after year. Pray again for Christ to come. But even more, hope to be struck to the core by just how much we need him to.

PRAYER

Make me feel my need for you, O Christ. Help me say, "Come!" And mean it.

When the Bad News is the Good News

Matt Laney

The day of the Lord will come like a thief, and then the heavens will pass away with a loud noise, and the elements will be dissolved with fire, and the earth and everything that is done on it will be disclosed. - 2 Peter 3:10 (NRSV)

Lewis and Clark were on an expedition.

At one point, Lewis said to his team, "Guys, I have good news and bad news. First, the good news: We covered 50 miles today, more than any other day on our entire trip! Now the bad news: We're lost."

There are many such "good news/bad news" jokes with a variety of scenarios. I'd like to add one more based on the text from 2 Peter.

Peter: "Church, I've got good news and more good news: The Day of the Lord is coming!"

Church: "Yay! And there's even more good news?"

Peter: "Yes! When the Lord returns, the heavens will vanish, everything on earth will be dissolved with fire and all of humanity's shameful deeds will be displayed on God's jumbotron! Can I get an amen?!"

Church: (crickets)

I don't associate the coming of Christ with seemingly bad news, definitely not in this season of good cheer. Yet, for the writer of 2 Peter, the bad news is the good news. Why? Because their church faced regular persecution and hardship. Word that Christ was coming to reveal and destroy the evils they deplored could not have been more welcome.

We are no different. When the daily news is bad, really bad, we quickly pray for its undoing, such as...

PRAYER

God, we feel lost among so much bad news: white supremacy, nationalism, authoritarianism, greed, falsehoods, pollution, pestilence, disease, hunger, addiction, violence, temperatures, wildfires, storms. May they all be destroyed when you appear. Soon please.

Hood and Holy

Naomi Washington-Leapheart

The Word became flesh and blood, and moved into the neighborhood. We saw the glory with our own eyes, the one-of-a-kind glory, like Father, like Son, generous inside and out, true from start to finish. - John 1:14 (The Message)

To me, the pandemic has felt like a cruel game of hide-and-seek with God. I didn't know I was "it," but since March 2020, I've found myself covering my eyes and counting cases, deaths, tears, and fears. When I get tired of counting and begin to search for God in all of it, I panic. I've looked under every rock and around every corner. Sometimes I find the residue of God's presence, but other times I find only chaos. Where is God?

So many of us have lamented the disruption that Covid-19 has been to our worship. Sure, God is everywhere, but God's home base is the sanctuary, right?

But as Shug Avery says to Celie in Alice Walker's epic novel, *The Color Purple:* "...have you ever found God in church? I never did. I just found a bunch of folks hoping for him to show. Any God I ever felt in church I brought in with me. And I think all the other folks did too. They come to church to share God, not find God."

God's home base is the neighborhood and God is the preeminent good neighbor. Picture it: God is on the front stoop, watching the kids jump double-dutch, waving at the mail carrier, listening to Frankie Beverly and Maze on repeat. God wants to be in the messiness of life with us, sighing with us as we sit in the idling car in the driveway after a long day of work, pacing the floor with us when we can't fall asleep, dancing with us as we fold laundry to our favorite tunes. Have you seen God in the neighborhood lately?

PRAYER

God, you know where we live! Thank you for moving in, not to displace or shame, but to share light and love and life. May our search for you always lead us home.

Thank you, God, for the witness
of Howard Thurman. Help us this
Advent to light your candles to
"burn all the year long."
Amen.

December 3, 2021

Candles in the Night

Talitha Arnold

"By the tender mercy of our God, the dawn from on high will break upon us, to give light to those who sit in darkness and in the shadow of death, to guide our feet into the way of peace." - Luke 1:78-79 (NRSV)

"I will light Candles this Christmas," wrote theologian Howard Thurman in a poem published after his death in 1981. "Candles of joy despite all sadness, candles of hope where despair keeps watch, candles of courage for fears ever present."

Like old Zechariah living under Roman oppression, Thurman knew only too well the shadows of his time. As an African-American boy growing up in Florida, he'd experienced first-hand the long night of segregation and the ever-present fear of racial violence. As an adult, he learned that racism and hatred weren't confined to one state or region. Thurman came of age during World War I when African Americans fought and died for their country, but then came home to a nation that still denied their full humanity. He was 19 when the flu pandemic broke out, exposing the country's chasms between class and race.

Yet also like Zechariah, Thurman knew the power of light to dispel the shadows of fear and despair. Connecting prayer and faith with resistance and social justice, he called Martin Luther King, Jr., Rosa Parks, John Lewis, and others in the Civil Rights movement to light their candles of courage and hope.

Thurman's poem continues to call us. May we light our Advent Candles to be, in his words, candles of "peace for tempest-tossed days, candles of grace to ease heavy burdens, candles of love to inspire all [our] living."

PRAYER

Thank you, God, for the witness of Howard Thurman. Help us this Advent to light your candles to "burn all the year long." Amen.

December 4, 2021

Hornblower

Quinn G. Caldwell

"Blessed be the Lord God of Israel, for she has looked favorably on his people and redeemed them. He has raised up a mighty savior for us in the house of his servant David."

- Luke 1:68-69 (NRSV)

Raising up a "mighty savior" would be a good reason to bless the Lord God of Israel, but actually, that's not what Zechariah says has happened. Translation issues; you know how it is. What he actually says is that God has raised up a "horn of salvation." Much more evocative. "Savior" slips right through our heads as if we know what it means (though we don't). But a horn of salvation? Like, what could that even be?

If you assume it refers to Jesus, as many do (see "mighty savior"), then it's pretty confusing. Is it, like, a horn on a goat's head? Is Jesus going to butt his way through the world? Possible; Jesus wasn't as gentle as some of us want to believe. But Jesus hasn't been born yet, and Zechariah is talking about this horn of salvation like it's already here.

On the other hand, Zechariah is currently holding his own son. The one who would grow up to become John the Baptist, the one who would point and announce and say, "Prepare ye the way." Like a herald, like a trumpeter. Like the shofar that echoed out of the cloud on Mt. Sinai, that brings walls crumbling to the ground, that can be heard echoing across the hills to marshal the people, that calls them to worship and repentance.

Not the savior, but the one who gets people to pay attention long enough to notice that the savior is here.

PRAYER

You and I know I can't save the world. But the horn of salvation is an instrument I'm willing to learn. Amen.

Really Ready

Kenneth L. Samuel

"The messenger of the covenant, whom you look for so eagerly, is surely coming," says the Lord of Heaven's Armies. "But who will be able to endure it when he comes? For he will be like a blazing fire that refines metal, or like a strong soap that bleaches clothes."

- Malachi 3:1-2 excerpts (NLT)

Have you ever been ready for something until you got it … and then found out you were not really ready for it at all? Sometimes what we think we really want comes with changes we didn't expect and are not prepared for.

Everyone who thinks they're ready for a pet may not be prepared to take care of one. The walks, the food, the medical care, the pet-sitting when you're away. All these things and more come along with the advent of pets.

Relationships, too, are much more than sentimental feelings. The constant communication and compromises require much more than sensual romantic episodes.

And many of the professional promotions we are so eager to attain place increased demands on our time and concentration.

With all our eager expectations, it behooves us to pause and consider what will be required of us when those expectations arrive. When our heart's desire is delivered, how will it change our hearts?

Advent is the time of joyous anticipation for the coming of the Messiah. But are we really ready?

Are we really ready to be purged from the dross of elaborate but empty religiosity? Are we really ready for a deep dive of the Spirit into our personal contradictions? Are we really ready to be bleached and scoured into a newness of life?

Much more than a glorious expectation, Advent requires real preparation.

PRAYER

"Fix me for my starry crown. Fix me Jesus, fix me. Fix me for a higher ground. Fix me Jesus, fix me."

December 6, 2021

Disoriented

A n n   K a n s f i e l d

"Blessed is the one whom God corrects; so do not despise the discipline of the Almighty. For God wounds, but God also binds up; God injures, but God's hands also heal. From six calamities God will rescue you; in seven no harm will touch you." - Job 5:17-19 (NIV)

Maybe it's Covid-tide, or just a mix up in my own daily rhythms, but somehow I've ended up disoriented from the tick-tick-tick of the calendar. Job 5:13-14 sums up my disorientation in time: "God catches the wise in their craftiness, and the schemes of the wily are swept away. Darkness comes upon them in the daytime; at noon they grope as in the night." It sure feels like darkness must have come in the day, and I ate lunch in the dark. What happened? Was I wily or just forgetful?

When such a disorientation happens, it's easy for me (and perhaps you, too?) to fall into a self-made pit of despair. My inner self-talk can quickly turn to blame and shame: "Why can't I remember when something is due!? Why did I wait for the last minute?!"

But the message in Job continues with some words of comfort for human beings—those of us who make human errors. Being corrected is a blessing. Don't be angry at God for receiving discipline; welcome it as a guide for your future. God protects you, there is nothing to fear. We all make mistakes. The key is to be open to correcting them and doing better the next time. God rescues us from calamities, even of our own making. And perhaps they aren't calamities at all, but merely opportunities for learning.

P R A Y E R

God, may your rhythms become my rhythms. May I not be afraid when you correct my ways and reorient me in your direction. Amen.

December 7, 2021

If, Then

Vicki Kemper

God, change our circumstances for the better, like dry streams in the desert waste! Let those who plant with tears reap the harvest with joyful shouts. Let those who go out crying and carrying their seed, come home with joyful shouts, carrying bales of grain.   - Psalm 126:4-6 (CEB)

If Advent is a good time to get in touch with our spiritual longings (it is), it is a great time to name exactly what we and the world need, to imagine the life that God intends, and to pray boldly for it.

This psalm shows us one way to do that, starting with the general—God, please make things better!—and then moving on to the specifics of what better would look like: Let those who started out weeping with little but hope in their hands end up shouting for joy, gladly bearing the bountiful fruits of their labors.

If Advent reminds us that God is doing yet another new thing and coming to us in still more unexpected ways (it does and She is), and if Advent invites us to prepare the way for newness (it does), then we'd best get ready to recognize and receive the unlikely and unimaginable answers to our prayers.

If you knew a friend was coming for a long-awaited visit, you'd clean the house and prepare the finest food and drink. If the weather worsened and the hour grew late, you'd turn on all the lights and pace the floor until you heard their knock on the door.

So let us make room in our hearts for the answers to our prayers. Let us live as if our Advent longings *will* be fulfilled.

PRAYER

I trust you are on your way. Let me be ready to receive you.

December 8, 2021

Daydream Believer

Rachel Hackenberg

When the Lord restored the fortunes of Zion, we were like those who dream. Then our mouths filled with laughter and our tongue with shouts of joy. - Psalm 126:1-2a (NRSV)

Is it better to dream or to be practical? To envision a new world, a just world, an honorable world … or to observe the world as it is without illusion?

I'm more of the latter sort. The "daydreaming won't make a hard day easier" sort. The "it doesn't make a difference whether you say 'half full' or 'half empty,' because either way you have half a cup" sort.

Not pessimistic. Realistic.

Except, of course, that I do dream.

I dream of peace. Of safety. Of well-being and joy. Of sowing and reaping purposefully, gratefully. Of stretching and relaxing and being—without a crick in my neck, a knot in my shoulder, and an anxious eye on my bank account.

Calling myself a realist is just a cover really, a ruse to avoid admitting that I expect to be disappointed by unrealized dreams.

Maybe you live that way, too—with the expectation of disappointment.

The season of Advent, then, becomes our time to practice daydreaming without hesitation, without skepticism or reluctance, without a backup plan in case of disappointment. The promise of Advent's dream has already been fulfilled! The experience of Advent's dream is already spelled out for us: Tears turning to laughter. Displaced people returning home. A shoot pushing up from a stump. A word becoming flesh.

In Advent, we dream without disappointment.

PRAYER

Here is my joy, O God—not conditional or tentative, but full and free. Here is the song on my tongue, O God, unburdened by doubt and bitterness. Here is my laughter, O God, as my mouth tastes the sweet goodness of your realized dream.

December 9, 2021

Waterworks

Donna Schaper

There was a priest named Zechariah, who belonged to the priestly order of Abijah. His wife was a descendant of Aaron, and her name was Elizabeth. - Luke 1:5 (NRSV)

Imagine being John the Baptist's mother. Or father.

Imagine, alternatively, what it was like to be the mother of a 25-year-old who overdosed and died, right after spending two great weeks with his family and assuring them all that he was drug-free. Or being my daughter when her two-year-old said she had eaten a water bead, the kind that expands to 40 times their size once placed in a balloon. (The child had not eaten the water bead but that was only proven after five hours in the emergency room, trying to decide about surgery, since water beads are translucent and don't necessarily come up on the x-ray.) We found the water beads, both of them, on the floor after returning from the emergency room. You can sign the online petition against this children's game. Or join my daughter in saying, "Jesus Crisis!"

Parents never know what is going to happen to their children. John the Baptist was beheaded, likely long after Elizabeth was gone. Or we certainly hope so.

But before he died an awful death, he "invented" baptism, a super-soaker ceremony if there ever was one. A water bead of a kind, capable of great magnification. Just water, we say. But then again, is there any water that is just water?

Albert Einstein is said to have said that there are two kinds of people, those who don't believe in miracles and those who think everything is a miracle. Mothers have to believe everything is a miracle. Why? Because like Elizabeth, like Mary, they watch their children grow.

PRAYER

Let us remember our baptism today and know that we are really and truly all wet, all miracle, all birthed. Amen.

I Need It to Be True

John Edgerton

Surely God is my salvation; I will trust and not be afraid. The Lord God is my strength and my defense; God has become my salvation. With joy you will draw water from the wells of salvation. - Isaiah 12:2-3 (NRSV)

Last summer, I led a graveside prayer service for a young person who was killed at just 15 years old. Before an open grave I spoke the old words again. "In the sure and certain hope of the resurrection to eternal life in Jesus Christ…"

I've spoken those words many times at the graveside. They are words of deepest hope and surest faith. And they are words only ever spoken from the depths of profoundest grief.

Our faith is like that. We speak our most beautiful and sturdy words only from the very worst depths.

Isaiah's words are the same. They are words of calm assurance spoken at a moment of profound national crisis, when the collapse of all that was good was just around the corner. Jesus' words are the same. The last are first and the lost are found and the way that leads to life runs through the heart of death's dread valley.

I can't understand any of it. Exegete as I might, study as I might, preach as I might, I can't understand it. How can such beauty shine amidst the ugliest heaps of reality? I can't understand it.

But I don't need to understand it. I need it to be true. Down deep in my bones, past my feelings, past my thoughts, past my understanding, at the very heart of what it means to live and die, I need it all to be true.

PRAYER

May the peace that passes all understanding attend all of us.

May the peace that passes all understanding attend all of us.

Shaken and Stirred

Lillian Daniel

"Let us consider how to stir up one another to love and good works ... and all the more as you see the Day drawing near." - Hebrews 10:24-25 (ESV)

"Here I am, with my hair all fallen out, months to live, and my only desire is to live to see my daughter graduate from high school," said the dying woman, reacting to the visitor who had just left as I walked in. "And this woman is sitting in my living room complaining because her kid got the wrong coach for travel soccer." No sooner had she invited me into her interior monologue, then she softened the story by saying, "I don't mean to sound insensitive. I used to care about those things too. I'd never say any of that out loud."

"But thank God you just did!" I said, for I needed a reminder that the dying know things the rest of us do not. For one thing, they know they are not immortal.

"If you could say anything, without fear of hurting our feelings, what would you say?" I asked, because I now realized that her last visitor could have been any one of us.

"Don't get so upset about the small things. Take notice of all that is good," she said. "But words don't really do it. Mostly, I just want to grab you all by the shoulders and shake you!"

"Consider me shaken and stirred," I replied. This amazing woman, so afraid of being insensitive, was no such thing. She was highly sensitive to the eternal truths that blasted away the banalities of life and exposed my secret worries for what they were—relatively small things—as the Day for us all draws near.

PRAYER

Holy Spirit, stir up your love in my living and your truth before my dying. Amen.

Good News?

Marilyn Pagán-Banks

John answered, "I baptize you with water; but one who is more powerful than I is coming; I am not worthy to untie the thong of his sandals. He will baptize you with the Holy Spirit and fire. His winnowing fork is in his hand, to clear his threshing floor and to gather the wheat into his granary; but the chaff he will burn with unquenchable fire." So, with many other exhortations, he proclaimed the good news to the people. - Luke 3:16-18 (NRSV)

Good news?! I guess it depends which side of the fork you are on. This is certainly not a vision of the baby born in a manger and wrapped in swaddling cloth.

John's idea of the Messiah was all about power and might and control. It is what the people wanted fter centuries of oppression and colonization. "Finally, some justice!" I imagine some thinking.

But instead of a winnowing fork, Jesus comes with open hands, inviting all into right relationship. A relationship grounded in a love so expansive it became flesh so we can feel it. Touch it. Allow it to transform us.

Jesus comes and offers living water to all. He offers the bread of life to all. Jesus reminds us that we, too, are sourced from this love. Made from it. And can live into it more fully. This love will make us free!

PRAYER

This is good news on this third Sunday of Advent, Immanuel, God with us. Thank you for this season of remembering, sharing the story, and inviting others into the possibility of your love. Amen.

December 13, 2021

Revealation

Matt Laney

Because you have kept my word of patient endurance, I will keep you from the hour of trial that is coming on the whole world to test the inhabitants of the earth. I am coming soon!

- Revelation 3:10-11 (NRSV)

If you've ever felt misunderstood, you know just how the book of Revelation has felt every day for two millennia. Revelation is the most misunderstood and misinterpreted book in the bible.

Few legit Bible scholars see Revelation as a roadmap for the future. (Also note that "antichrist" and "the rapture" are not mentioned.) Instead, Revelation offered hope and encouragement to a specific group of first century, persecuted, fearful Christians. "Hang in there, Christ-followers!" it said. "Holy help is on the way!"

In our time, the book of Revelation is well-suited to preachers like the Rev. Allan Boesak from South Africa, who preached on Revelation during apartheid. Boesak's parishioners knew what it was like to live each day as if it were their last.

Today, the Rev. William Barber II, founder of Moral Mondays and the Poor People's Campaign, regularly invokes images from Revelation to decry the ills of capitalism and the legacy of slavery while announcing protection for the marginalized.

If the book of Revelation feels more harrowing than hopeful, it might have something to do with our social location. Revelation not only reveals an ancient people in peril, it reveals us now. As the saying goes, it comforts the afflicted and afflicts the comfortable.

PRAYER

God of Revelation, before I dismiss something that makes me uncomfortable, help me face what it reveals about me.

December 14, 2021

Protect the Herd

Kaji Douša

"See, I am sending you out like lambs into the midst of wolves." - Isaiah 11:6 (NRSV)

Armed with nothing but the peace they offer, Jesus sends the disciples out almost as prey, knowing that the wolves would pack up and attack.

How, lamb, do you offer peace to a wolf?

I'll be honest. I'd prefer not to be the lamb in this situation. Maybe a direwolf. Or a bear might suit me better.

But disciples don't get to fight back in kind. They have to offer peace. We have to offer peace.

Was Jesus naïve? I don't think so. It's clear he knew that in many cases his peace would be rejected. That many a wolf couldn't look past the lamb being a lamb, even though that lamb would bear precisely what the wolf needed.

You may be a disciple.

But you're not the only one.

There are other lambs.

And if we're doing our job, then the people with whom we interact will encounter another lamb in due time. And maybe something of the cumulative effect of the peace we attempt to give will change things.

Until the day when Isaiah's vision comes true—that the wolf lies down with the lamb—we'll only get glimpses of when this isn't adversarial.

But those glimpses are worth it.

Because hearts must change and the gospel must be preached.

PRAYER

Strengthen us, O God, and may the protection of the herd be clear and present. Amen.

God of all creation, your prophet called us to neither harm nor destroy anything on your holy mountain.

December 15, 2021

Where the Wild Things Aren't

Talitha Arnold

The wolf shall live with the lamb, the leopard shall lie down with the kid, the calf and the lion and the fatling together, and a little child shall lead them. The cow and the bear shall graze, their young shall lie down together; and the lion shall eat straw like the ox.

- Isaiah 11:6-7 (NRSV)

Until a few years ago, I delighted in Isaiah's "peaceable kingdom" with its vision of an abundant and playful creation, filled with lions and lambs, leopards and little goats, bears and cows all getting along.

But then I learned that the Syrian brown bear, which roamed from northern Lebanon down to the Sinai in Isaiah's time, is essentially extinct throughout the Middle East. Habitat loss from endless wars has taken its toll, as have deforestation and poaching. A handful of zoos and private preserves still hold a few bears, but none exist in the wild.

Similarly, until last century, Arabian leopards thrived in the region's mountains and deserts. With less than 200 of the big cats left, they are now considered critically endangered. The region's wolf population has met a similar fate. Even the Lion of Judah, aka the Asiatic lion, has vanished from the landscape.

Given our human role in the extinction of so many of God's creatures, whether in the Middle East or in our own country, I wonder what Isaiah's peaceable kingdom would look like now. He promised that a "little child shall lead them," but I pray we don't leave to the next generation the work of repairing the damage we've done.

PRAYER

God of all creation, your prophet called us to neither harm nor destroy anything on your holy mountain. We have done both. We ask your forgiveness and pray for the commitment and courage to help restore your creation. Amen.

Headlines and Lowlights

Martha Spong

But this is the covenant that I will make with the house of Israel after those days, says the Lord: I will put my law within them, and I will write it on their hearts; and I will be their God, and they shall be my people. - Jeremiah 31:33 (NRSV)

I don't know why I keep looking at the news first thing every morning. For a long time, I thought knowing what was happening in the world, even the worst of it, would make me feel more secure, better prepared to respond to disaster. But a lot of the time—maybe even most of the time—I end up feeling unsettled instead, frustrated by the number of things that feel out of control and mad at the people who are making them that way.

I hear my father's voice from long ago telling me, "Don't say mad, say angry." But this feeling I have goes way beyond angry. It's as if all my joints are both wound up tight and impossibly loose. I have the passion to smash things but none of the precision to keep from being reckless. And while, if pressed, I would tell you I don't believe in an actual Devil, that feeling and the people and situations that inspire it feel like hell.

My lowlights correspond with the lowlights of the world as it is. When we get caught in the hellmouth of headlines, we fix nothing and help no one.

Maybe today, I'll leave my phone on the bedside table and turn to a different authority for my security. Maybe today, instead, I will embrace the early morning and pray.

PRAYER

Holy God, write your law on our hearts. Bring about the world as it should be, for everyone. Amen.

The Perfect Gift

Chris Mereschuk

Every good gift, every perfect gift, comes from above. - James 1:17 (CEB)

My mother paints rocks she finds on the beach near her home, decorating them with landscapes, lighthouses, hearts, and flowers. Once she has a few ready, she'll take them back to the beach and give them away, leaving them on fenceposts and car door handles, tossing them on beach towels and into people's bags. She doesn't know who receives the rocks, and the recipient doesn't know who gave it to them. There's no expectation of reciprocity, nothing transactional. My mom gets to share her art, and someone gets a random gift.

In a way, this is a perfect gift. But it's harder to get a gift for someone you know.

Finding the perfect gift can be a real struggle. Coming up with the right thing, how much to spend, will they like it? We want to give the perfect gift.

Receiving gifts can be just as fraught. Expectations, not wanting people to spend money on us, disappointment. We want to receive the perfect gift.

But if every truly good and perfect gift comes from God above, then maybe we give from the Spirit of God that is within: love, service, patience, forgiveness, compassion, accompaniment, the present of presence. These gifts will always be in stock, always in fashion, free shipping, the perfect size, and personal.

These perfect gifts still have a cost: giving of ourselves and our time, setting aside fear of scarcity or rejection, vulnerability, courage, effort, and intention.

Yes, there is a cost. But these perfect gifts are priceless.

PRAYER

Holy One, thank you for these perfect gifts. Compel us to share them generously and freely, and to humbly accept these gifts when given in return. Amen.

December 18, 2021

2 Legit 2 Quit

Phiwa Langeni

God gives a hand to those down on their luck, gives a fresh start to those ready to quit.

- Psalm 145 (MSG)

In 1991, Hammer released his hit song, "2 Legit 2 Quit." The only lyrics I know are in the title, which was sufficient apparently. During the unintelligible parts, the song's music and energy always coaxed my body to dance (not quite like Hammer, though my efforts were noble). When the chorus arrived, I'd boisterously belt out, "Too legit to quit!" That title phrase became a steady part of my language diet. Indeed, my peers and I often expressed it with the accompanying hand motions. Years beyond popularity, the phrase became a mantra that carried me through rough times.

I recently watched the celebrity-filled, over-fourteen-minute music video. It begins with a mock news bulletin announcing that Hammer's quitting. The newscaster speculates, "I know why he quit. He doesn't know who he is." Later, questioning his own readiness, Hammer approaches the Godfather of Soul, James Brown, who hurls flames of energy into Hammer's body and says, "Now you've received the gift. Go out and give it all you've got!" For the remainder of the video, Hammer performs the song while energy flames emerge from him and spread around the world, gifting it to others.

As we await Jesus' arrival, let's glean wisdom from this catchy throwback. No matter what people say about you, remember who you are—a legitimate image of God—so you don't quit. No matter how ill-equipped or insecure you feel, receive the Gift, infused into every part of your being, then "go out and give it all you've got!"

PRAYER

Praying with James Brown's words, "Never give up. Never quit. Because you're [Divinely] too legit to quit." Amen.

Imagining Gutsy Mary

Mary Luti

Mary said, "My soul magnifies my God; for you have looked with favor on the lowliness of your servant. You have brought down the powerful from their thrones, and lifted up the lowly; you have filled the hungry, and sent the rich away empty." - Luke 1:47-48 & 52-53 (NRSV, adapted)

In this song, Mary calls herself "lowly." Which doesn't mean "humble" or "meek." It means "poor." It's not a metaphor. Mary was poor, dirt poor. She sings about God's new world in the way poor people always have, in the midst of life's hard grief. She feels its joy while up to her neck in privation, which is, perhaps, the only place where such imagination is even possible.

It takes imagination to sing about a new world in the midst of the violence and pain of the old. No matter when or where, it also takes guts to sing of the powerful dethroned, of poor bellies filled. It's like a raised fist. Try doing it in the boardroom of Amazon. The gift is not welcome everywhere.

Mary's got guts, and she's pregnant with imagination. Pregnant with a Child. And like pregnant women, she dares to believe that it's God's new world growing in her womb, that her child will one day make all the difference.

You don't have to be pregnant to imagine like Mary. But we can't imagine at all if we won't relinquish our privilege and confess that things aren't the way God intends, and that we're part of the problem. If we can't contain our avarice to receive the dream with uncluttered hearts. If we never find true solidarity with the dirt poor, with Marys everywhere.

And if we can't imagine, we can't hope. And if we can't hope, we'll only fear. And if there's only fear, we know what that does to us and where it leaves us, where it's always left the world.

PRAYER

We want to hope. We want a new world. Give the church, give me, the guts and imagination of Mary.

December 20, 2021

At Work in the World

Vicki Kemper

God said to Rebekah, "Two nations are in your womb; two different peoples will emerge from your body." … When she reached the end of her pregnancy, she discovered she had twins.

- Genesis 25:23-24 (CEB)

Christ is the image of the invisible God, the firstborn of all creation, for in him all things in heaven and on earth were created. In him all the fullness of God was pleased to dwell, and through him God was pleased to reconcile to Godself all things.

- Colossians 1:15-20, excerpted (NRSV)

Long before Esau and Jacob were born, eons before they fought in Rebekah's womb and grew up to fight for Isaac's blessing, ages before one twin cheated the other and had to run for his life, there was a cosmic force at work in the world to heal, restore, and redeem all people and all creation.

Long before a baby named Jesus was born in Bethlehem and grew up to be a barrier-crossing, trouble-making, lowly-lifting, death-defying wonder, there was a dynamic force working in and through all things to love, heal, and reconcile all people and creation.

As the stories of Jacob and Esau and Jesus of Nazareth remind us, the workings of this transformative love rarely follow a straight line. The ordained, ever-in-process healing, reconciliation, and peace is usually less "Kumbaya" or "Silent Night" than trouble in the streets, struggles for justice, and life-giving lessons learned the hard way.

Incarnation is a messy, dangerous, wondrous business. And while we celebrate the Word Become Flesh once a year, the reconciling Christ always has been and always will be at work in the world.

PRAYER

Whatever our situation, may we trust that your love is at work in it.

December 21, 2021

Sitting High...Looking Low

Kenneth L. Samuel

Who is like the Lord our God, the One who sits enthroned on high, who stoops down to look on the heavens and the earth? He raises the poor from the dust and lifts the needy from the ash heap. - Psalm 113:5-7 (NIV)

About six years ago, our church sponsored a youth trip to our nation's capital. While touring the capital buildings, we ran into Congressman John Lewis. The Congressman John Lewis. The Civil Rights icon. The Presidential Medal of Freedom recipient. The moral conscience of the U.S. Congress.

We had no appointment with the Congressman, and our church is not located in his district. But upon introducing myself and our youth group, he invited us (a group of 30) to his office. His staff scrambled to find chairs for all of us and supplied us with plenty of Georgia peanuts, fruit, and water.

Then we listened as Congressman Lewis talked to us about how our nation has been lifted through the rich contributions and profound sacrifices of those who fight for racial equality. We looked at pictures of the Congressman leading historic marches and shaking hands with presidents, celebrities, and several world leaders. Then the Congressman answered questions from the youth and challenged them to give their best in every struggle for justice.

I've often reflected on how amazing our time with Congressman Lewis was.

Greatness and accessibility are not usually in sync in our society. The greater a person's elevation, the less available they become to everyday people.

The psalmist tells us God's throne is so high that God stoops down to reach the heavens above. And God stoops even further to gaze upon the earthly affairs of you and me, with love and compassion.

PRAYER

Thank you, Lord, for the high exaltation and the lowly compassion exemplified in your advent. Amen.

Is That Your Cat?

Lillian Daniel

Show hospitality to one another without grumbling. - 1 Peter 4:9 (ESV)

When the temperature dropped in Iowa, a stray skinny alley cat cried and shivered outside our backdoor, so we started setting out a bit of food. We posted her picture online to see if anyone had lost a teenage tabby with a big appetite, but no one claimed her, and eventually she claimed us. After a vet visit and microchip marked her as ours, we named her Hildegard. She discovered the joy of sleeping inside but she would never be a house cat. Each morning, for the last three years, she has patrolled the perimeter of our urban jungle, protecting her home from skunks, snakes, and an obstinate groundhog who appears to be in love with her.

Just the other day, as we sat on the front porch, a couple stopped their walk and pointed to Hildegard, who was keeping watch from the railing like a jaguar, one paw hanging down. "Is that your cat?" the man asked, as Hildegard perked up at the sound of his voice. We assured him she was, and he said, "Well, my wife's been feeding that cat every morning!"

Suddenly Hildegard plopped to the sidewalk with an audible thud that revealed she had indeed been getting a little chunky. As the man tickled her stomach and cooed to her in their own special language, the scope of Hildegard's betrayal hit me. All this time, she had another secret family!

For a minute there, I wanted to take back all the hospitality, take back all the affection, and definitely take back all the vet bills. But that's not how hospitality works. It is supposed to abundant.

Hildegard found it everywhere and that's the way God wants it.

PRAYER

As the birth of Jesus approaches, remind me to show hospitality without grumbling and without keeping score. Amen.

As the birth of Jesus approaches, remind me to show hospitality without grumbling and without keeping score. Amen.

December 23, 2021

Heritable

Quinn G. Caldwell

Mary said, "God's mercy is for those who fear God from generation to generation."

- Luke 1:50 (NRSV)

In the winter of 1944-45, a German blockade in the occupied Netherlands cut off shipments of food and other necessities. The resulting famine is known as the Hunger Winter. After its end, The Dutch Famine Birth Cohort Study famously followed the survivors. It and subsequent studies discovered that children of those who were pregnant during the Hunger Winter were more likely to have a whole range of health problems, from diabetes to schizophrenia to heart disease and more. Not only that, there is evidence to suggest that the grandchildren of survivors also have higher rates of a variety of illnesses. The descendants have all the food they need, but they're famine-struck nevertheless.

Intergenerational trauma is real. PTSD is heritable. For the sins done to their fathers, children suffer not just behaviorally but phenotypically. Grandchildren bear the epigenetic scars and hungers of their grandparents.

Jesus' mother Mary had been through plenty of trauma and was betting there'd be more. It's no accident she sang these words while she was pregnant. She knew her son would be born with her bruises; she was determined to pass God's grace on as well.

The Bible is preoccupied with God's constancy through the generations. The writers want to be sure you know that God is here with mercy for you in the midst of whatever befalls you in your lifetime. But they also want to be sure you know that God was there when the thing happened to your grandfather that's shaping you now. God will be there, too, if your child is born with your wounds.

Damage can last generations. God knows that grace is only helpful if it does, too.

PRAYER

For intergenerational salvation, for heritable grace, thank you. Amen.

Registration

Rachel Hackenberg

In those days a decree went out from Emperor Augustus that all the world should be registered. This was the first registration and was taken while Quirinius was governor of Syria. ... Joseph went to be registered with Mary, to whom he was engaged and who was expecting a child. - Luke 2:1-2 & 5 (NRSV)

In those days, households were required to register with their provinces for the purpose of being taxed by the Roman Empire. Some complied. Some resisted. Some fled. Some revolted against a headcount that served only to extract money from oppressed communities.

In these days, adults working in the U.S. are required to register with the Social Security Administration for the purpose of paying taxes. For some adults, compliance begins with the registration of a Social Security Number. For others who are barred from registration, non-compliance is necessary for working and living.

In these days, photo identification cards are frequently required to purchase prescriptions, pick up packages, drive a motor vehicle, or pay with a check. Many comply. Some resist, as photo IDs represent an infraction upon their religious beliefs.

In these days, proof of vaccination is increasingly required to work, to attend school, to travel, to dine or to dance. Some are complying. Some are resisting. Some are seeking exemption.

In these days, as in those days, required registrations shape our lives—no matter if we comply or resist.

In those days, as in these days, God's work within, through, around, and beyond us continues without fail—no matter our registration status.

PRAYER

God Most Holy, God Made Flesh, navigating all these social regulations and government registrations is a daily spiritual exercise. On this holy eve, we wait in expectation for the Miracle that unfolds within—yet is unhindered by—the demands of this world.

Our soul magnifies you, O God.
May we heed the words of the prophets
of yesterday, today, and tomorrow.

The Prophet Mary

Kaji Douša

God has brought down rulers from their thrones but has lifted up the humble. - Luke 1:52 (NIV)

Mary has words. Strong words. Prophetic words. Because—do realize—this was a prophecy.

After Gabriel's troubling visit, reflecting on what God has done with the announcement of this child she will bear, Mary has a vision.

But the road towards it will be perilous.

The ruler on the throne will persecute her family. He will force them out of the country.

In hot pursuit of Jesus, the king will round up all of the male children under 2 years old. He will massacre these innocent children. Babies.

No doubt the Prophet Mary saw the king's potential to do such a horrific thing.

Prophets see into the future and proclaim God's will.

Would that it doesn't take millennia to realize it.

PRAYER

Our soul magnifies you, O God. May we heed the words of the prophets of yesterday, today, and tomorrow.

In Case You're Crying on a Twin Bed at Your Parents' House at Any Point Today

Vince Amlin

As God's chosen ones, holy and beloved, clothe yourselves with compassion, kindness, humility, meekness, and patience. Bear with one another and, if anyone has a complaint against another, forgive each other. ... Above all, clothe yourselves with love, which binds everything together in perfect harmony. - Colossians 3:12-14 (NRSV)

Whoever chose this reading for the day after Christmas must have known. You don't just accidentally pick a scripture that says "bear with one another" for the #1 day when such advice is needed.

When the kids have nothing left to unwrap and turn to other forms of destruction. When siblings slip back into roles they thought they gave up decades ago. When the loaded comments you overlooked yesterday to keep things merry start to wear on you. When uncles turn to politics. When cousins get religious.

Colossians reads like the pep talk you deliver in a whisper after you roll off the mostly deflated air mattress: "Let's rise to the occasion, clothe ourselves with love, and we'll leave after lunch." Whoever chose it must have known.

And God knows too.

That's what it means to worship a God who became human. They know. They get it. They've been there. They are there. With you. Right now. On the air mattress. Trying to remember what your therapist said. White-knuckling your sobriety. Crying in your childhood bedroom.

God knows.

So, holy and beloved ones, when you've blown your nose and your eyes aren't so puffy, go join the *Monopoly* game that has not yet become a fight. Bear with one another. Forgive each other. Clothe yourselves with love. And leave after lunch.

PRAYER

God, you know how it is. Thank you.

December 27, 2021

And the Worst Penmanship Award Goes To…

John Edgerton

See what large letters I make when I am writing in my own hand! - Galatians 6:11 (NRSV)

Manuscripts in the ancient world were weird. They would be all in one consistent, compact, neat set of handwriting. There would be no punctuation. There wouldn't even be spaces between words.

ImaginewhatreadingthatmusthavebeenlikeNotverymuchfunisit

Why write this way? The answer is totally pedestrian. Because paper was expensive. It might be leather, or imported materials made from specially processed Nile-delta reeds. A far cry from popping down to the supply closet for a ream of 8.5 x 11.

With that in mind, this dashed-off verse of Galatians tells us something interesting. Paul has taken over from the professional scribe in order to write in his own handwriting. The reader could immediately tell it was Paul writing because … well … he had lousy penmanship.

Why have Paul write at all? Because the intimacy of Paul's own handwriting was more important than getting every last detail perfectly, precisely on point. Production value is a good thing, and so is authenticity and intimacy.

So here's a shoutout to everyone—clergy and laity—who spent so much time in the past two years unexpectedly becoming videographers. Here's to the hours spent editing videos and singing with one earbud in for the virtual choir. Here's to porch drops and hours spent on the phone to find an inflatable movie screen for drive-in church. Here's to every last one of you who rolled with it and found ways to make it work.

Was it as perfect as Hollywood? No, it was so much more authentic and intimate. Don't take my word for it. Saint Paul and his big ol' loopy letters have been smiling down on us all along.

PRAYER

Thank you, God, for the joy of worshiping in new ways.

Another Way

Donna Schaper

"Herod is about to search for the child, to destroy him." - Matthew 2:13 (NRSV)

Mary and Joseph had to return home another way because Herod was after their baby. Thank God for their dreams.

The best book I have read in a very long time is by Ta-Nehisi Coates, *The Water Dancer.* It is a story about the underground railroad, about dreams, about flight, and how Herod doesn't win. Hiram tells a long story of losing his mother as she tries to escape slavery. He becomes the aid to "Moses." They are always going home another way, tricking their would-be masters over and over again. They even swim across the Delaware River at Philadelphia. They follow a great conduction. Their path becomes clear after they take their steps, not before. They experience what Jesus experienced as a baby: protection by way of dream and dreaming!

They made possible witness stones, like those in front of the First Congregational Church of Old Lyme, Connecticut. These read:

Cato Enslaved Servant, Child
By Rev. Jonathan Parsons,
Died here 1734, age 10.

Lewis Lewia, 1779 – 1852
Baptized age 16 in 1795.

Down the road in Guilford, Connecticut, there is a sign for the Third Congregational Church, long gone, but attesting that it split off from the others over abolition.

All these people join Coates in knowing about Herod and how, generation after generation, we outwit him by going home another way.

Perhaps you have had a dream that tells you to change course? To conduct change? To go underground? To split? To cover your tracks? To take another way? I sure have, over and over again.

PRAYER

Conduct us, O God, in the ways you would have us go. Keep testing our path, every day, every way. Amen.

Identity Crisis

Martha Spong

According to the grace of God given to me, like a skilled master builder I laid a foundation, and someone else is building on it. Each builder must choose with care how to build on it. For no one can lay any foundation other than the one that has been laid; that foundation is Jesus Christ. - 1 Corinthians 3:10-11 (NRSV)

Last Christmas morning, after leading worship on Zoom from my house, in my pajamas, I thought, "Well, we've done it! We've gotten through the hard time, the loneliest Christmas, the weirdest situation we could possibly imagine." I let myself imagine better times ahead: reunion, regathering, re-creation. I pictured it all rebuilt on the familiar foundation of pew Bibles and printed hymnals and offering plates passed up and down the pews, of candles lit and blown out, of bread broken and shared, of loved faces the same as ever except the children would be taller.

I let myself imagine it for a minute or three. It felt cozy and safe. But it did not feel right.

What are we making of the church now? Whether the people who came before us used old-growth lumber to raise high-ceilinged sanctuaries with beautiful acoustics or 1950s cinderblocks to build as many classrooms as they could afford, they showed us what mattered to them. Whatever our churches are becoming will never be a return to old ways. Does that sound like more than you signed up for? It may feel like an identity crisis, but I'd like to think it's a gorgeous opportunity to build something new on the surest foundation there is, choosing the materials with care, for the purpose God is showing us.

PRAYER

Everlasting God, may we build up faith communities that serve you. Amen.

Lord keep me alert to my past
and present so I can consciously
be better prepared for what's coming.
Amen.

December 30, 2021

Staying Woke

Kenneth L. Samuel

"Therefore, keep watch because you do not know when the owner of the house will come back. ... If he comes suddenly, do not let him find you sleeping. What I say to you, I say to everyone: 'Watch!'" - Mark 13:35-37 (NIV)

Being "woke" has become the new punchline that many social conservatives use to ridicule social progressives. In the minds of some, "woke culture" is now the pejorative label attached to everything from police reform to transgender equality.

But Jesus wasn't flippant or dismissive at all regarding the need for his listeners to stay conscious and alert in regard to the imminent changes occurring in their environment, in their society, and in their religious paradigm. Jesus did not want these changes to find his followers asleep on the eve of cosmic reconstruction.

If we had been more consciously alert to the scientific research and forecasts of global pandemics, we would have been better prepared to take the precautions necessary to save lives and mitigate much of the crisis we've endured over the past year and a half.

If we had been more consciously alert to the documented history of racism in America, we wouldn't find ourselves in so many volatile debates about critical race theory.

If we had been more consciously alert to the ill effects of global warming on our planet, we may not be battling incessant wildfires and intensified storms as we are today.

The handwriting on the wall cannot be read by those who are asleep. Prevention requires conscientious pro-activity.

The song, "Sweet Little Jesus Boy," is a bitter-sweet lament of our utter unpreparedness for Jesus' first Advent. May this lament not continue to be our epithet.

PRAYER

Lord keep me alert to my past and present so I can consciously be better prepared for what's coming. Amen.

Cry Out Now

Chris Mereschuk

For a long time I have held my peace, I have kept still and restrained myself; now I will cry out like one who is in labor. - Isaiah 42:14 (NRSV, adapted)

There's a sense of labor-weary impatience as one year nears its full term and the new one aches for birth. The approaching flip of the calendar compels us to tally the highs and lows, review our successes, leave behind our missteps and embarrassments, and resolve to do better and try it all again next year.

Why do we wait until the new year to do what we could do on any day?

Yes, some things must be allowed to gestate and fully form before they can be brought into being. And it's good to set intentions and look to a future date for restart and renewal.

But when we hold our peace to keep the peace, not wanting to upset the status quo or make others (ourselves) uncomfortable, things grow and build until the inevitable crisis bursts forth. We restrain ourselves to tiny whimpers and whines until we let out a loud cry, alerting others to our distress, demanding to be heard, or lamenting our own brokenness.

We do not need to wait for a new year to turn our hearts, make ourselves heard, seek justice, birth something new, or cry out. It is one thing to await the right time. It is another to restrain ourselves to our own detriment—and often to the detriment of others.

Don't wait for a crisis. Cry out now.

PRAYER

El Shaddai, we need you to be our midwife as we labor daily to birth something new. Hear our cries and attune our hearts to hear the cries of others. Amen.

A Radical Resolution

Ann Kansfield

I have seen the business that God has given to everyone to be busy with. God has made everything suitable for its time; moreover God has put a sense of past and future into their minds, yet they cannot find out what God has done from the beginning to the end.

- Ecclesiastes 3:10-11 (NRSV)

My family lives a block from Times Square. From our window, we can see "half" the ball drop. Actually, what we see is the number 20. A tall building blocks our view of the year–so we have to trust that it moved from 2021 to 2022 last night.

I like to think of time as one aspect of God's creation. It is too wonderful and mysterious to fully comprehend. Sometimes I'll look out the window and imagine that it's a different year: remembering a time in the past or dreaming about what it might be like far into the future.

Hey–as long as the year starts with 20, anything is possible with our view of the ball drop. It could be 2001 or 2099 for all we know. Time itself is so broad and deep and wide for me to begin to understand it. I'm in awe of astrophysicists who seem to understand so much more than I might imagine.

God has "made everything suitable for its time." Today we begin 2022. God has made everything suitable for today. Even the astrophysicists can't fully know what God has done from the beginning to the end. For today, we can rest in the assurance that God is present with us. You can resolve to be present in the moment today–neither yearning for the past or planning for the future. Perhaps that's the most radical of resolutions.

PRAYER

Thank you, God, for the mystery of time. Be present with me today as I seek to be present with you. Amen.

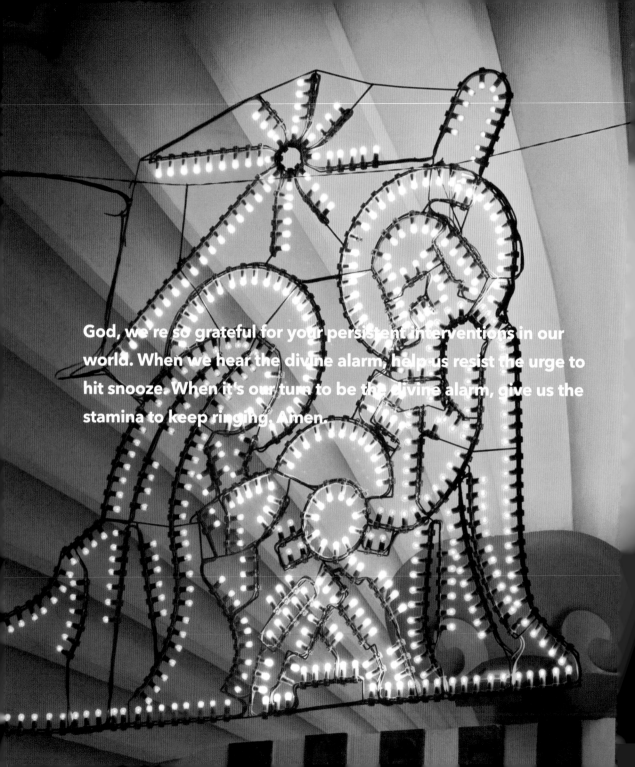

God, we're so grateful for your persistent interventions in our world. When we hear the divine alarm, help us resist the urge to hit snooze. When it's our turn to be the divine alarm, give us the stamina to keep ringing. Amen.

Being the Alarm

Naomi Washington-Leapheart

May the Lord God of Israel be blessed indeed! For God's intervention has begun, and God has moved to rescue us, the people of God. … And you, my son, will be called the prophet of the Most High. For you will be the one to prepare the way for the Lord, so that the Lord's people will receive knowledge of their freedom through the forgiveness of their sins. All this will flow from the kind and compassionate mercy of our God. A new day is dawning: the Sunrise from the heavens will break through in our darkness, and those who huddle in night, those who sit in the shadow of death, will be able to rise and walk in the light, guided in the pathway of peace. - Luke 1:68 & 76-79 (VOICE)

Let's be honest: nobody ever wants to be John the Baptist. He's the prophet with the street corner address, wild eyes, and odd smell. He points to a mystery others ridicule. Even his followers cannot protect him from state execution.

It's like that, though, for those who are the first to know that change is coming. They are the sensitive canaries who risk suffocation in order to signal what is to come. They are the ones called to fly close enough to bear witness to the rising Sun/Son.

Bishop Yvette Flunder often says, "The only difference between a heretic and a prophet is time." She's right. I wonder: can we rejoice, like Zechariah did, about the dawn of God's intervention, even if it means people will point, stare, doubt, and ignore now and believe later?

PRAYER

God, we're so grateful for your persistent interventions in our world. When we hear the divine alarm, help us resist the urge to hit snooze. When it's our turn to be the divine alarm, give us the stamina to keep ringing. Amen.

This Little Light of God's

Liz Miller

"No one after lighting a lamp hides it under a jar, or puts it under a bed, but puts it on a lampstand, so that those who enter may see the light." - Luke 8:16 (NRSV)

Every sermon I have ever heard, or preached, about letting your light shine was embedded with a set of instructions, calling the listener to figure out their gifts, put them to good use in the world, and shine as bright as they can.

There is nothing wrong with that message once in a while, but a lifetime of my favorite biblical metaphor telling me to "Go! Do! Shine!" makes me feel like I'm a 40-watt bulb shining in a 100-watt world.

I worry that I won't live up to the gifts I've been given or that trying to have the brightest light will make me burn out. Will I still be loved if I push the dimmer switch on my lamp once in a while and unplug from the world?

The part all those well-meaning calls to action miss is that it's not my light or your light. It is God's light. What a relief for all those times when my bulb threatens to come loose from its socket. How easy to forget that God is our source of energy. I know that God is strong enough that even if my bulb is a little dull, or in need of changing, God's light will find a way to shine.

PRAYER

Hey God, remember that time your light found its way through a tiny baby in Bethlehem? May it find its way through me, too. Amen.

Callused Hearts

Phiwa Langeni

"And you continue, so bullheaded! Calluses on your hearts, flaps on your ears! Deliberately ignoring the Holy Spirit, you're just like your ancestors." - Acts 7:51 (MSG)

Maneuvering the monkey bars on the playground as a child is one of my most amazing athletic feats to date. There's no way to fully describe how I felt when I could finally jump high enough to reach the bars from the ground without assistance. Or when I successfully moved from one bar to the next, making my way across the entire distance in one fell swoop and eventually learning daring tricks. American Ninja Warrior? Pssh. I was unstoppable!

The prolonged pressure from hanging on the bars and frequent friction from swinging across them created protective layers over the tender parts of my hand where my palms end and before my fingers begin. The more I played on the bars, the harder the calluses became. Like many children before me, my hardened skin became a badge of honor that I wore proudly. Those calluses remained until middle school when the playground grew up and no longer had monkey bars. Slowly, my palm skin softened with time to rest and heal.

Beyond the playground, we face exponentially more pressures to achieve success and more frictions that have us bullheadedly protecting our hearts. Calluses form, hardening this life-sustaining muscle that requires flexibility to function. Indeed, we must disrupt our inherited need to persist without rest so the internal and external healing we need can begin. Our lives depend on it.

PRAYER

Palliate the pressures that distort our suffering as badges of honor. Free us from the frictions that distance us from you and each other. Soften our hearts, protective God, so that we might deliberately recognize your presence in and all around us. Amen.

January 5, 2022

Not Unique

Quinn G. Caldwell

**In the beginning was the Word, and the Word was with God and the Word was God. …
And the Word became flesh and lived among us.** - John 1:1 & 14 (NRSV

Matthew wants to convince you that Jesus is descended from Abraham, by way of a lot of interesting saints and scalawags. Luke goes further, all the way back to Adam. John, who always has to do The Most, goes (*cue movie voiceover voice*) all the way back … to the beginning of time.

Nothingness. Then a tiny point of light. Then galaxies whirling into the void, pink and purple clouds expanding beyond imagination, stars growing and exploding and disappearing as they hurtle along. And after an age—or a thousand—whatever it was that was there watching when there was nothing to watch begins to move toward one spinning blue dot. Faster and faster—warp speed, streaks of light, full plaid—until it gets to the earth, enters geosynchronous orbit, hears the words, "Let it be with me according to your word," descends, enters.

John's always so over the top. And why not? Just because it's cinematic doesn't mean it didn't happen. And also: is this actually making any claims for Jesus that can't be made of you? Don't get me wrong: elsewhere John absolutely makes claims for Jesus he wouldn't make for you or me. But this part? About the power that was there at the beginning showing up on earth, climbing into a body made of history and the stuff of the universe? Is that actually different in any meaningful way from your own birth?

Some stories matter because they're about unique people. Some stories matter because they're about everybody.

PRAYER

For the utterly cosmic miracle that each one of us is, thank you.

Popular Wisdom

Marilyn Pagán-Banks

When they saw that the star had stopped, they were overwhelmed with joy. On entering the house, they saw the child with Mary his mother; and they knelt down and paid him homage. - Matthew 2:10-11 (NRSV)

Dare I bring up what happened last year? Of course! I don't believe anyone will ever think of Epiphany and not remember the shocking and violent event that took place on the Nation's Capital on January 6, 2021.

I hope we remember not simply to "stay stuck in our politics" or "hold on to trauma," but to observe, reflect and learn. To do better and to be different. To expect and accept accountability. To continue healing, growing, and building. So that we can do the work of ending hate and building the beloved community.

This is why we repeat the biblical stories: so we can recall, remember, and recommit ourselves as followers of Christ. So we can learn from the lived experience, popular wisdom and even human horrors found in these stories, and perhaps try to locate ourselves in them as we seek direction from yesterday's harms and for today's challenges.

God wants us to live, heal, have joy, and be love—and will stop at nothing to make sure we experience it. The entire universe is conspiring on our behalf! Are we paying attention to the signs? Are we open to God's disruptive Spirit calling us to new possibilities? Are we ready to let go of our fear and privilege? To own our place and collective power? To listen to our dreams and allow the universe to guide us? To pay homage to the love and gifts among us? Within us?

PRAYER

Thank you, Creator, for wisdom from unexpected places. We are grateful for the stars that guide the night, dreams that inspire and protect us, and your son that leads us in love and power. Amen and selah.

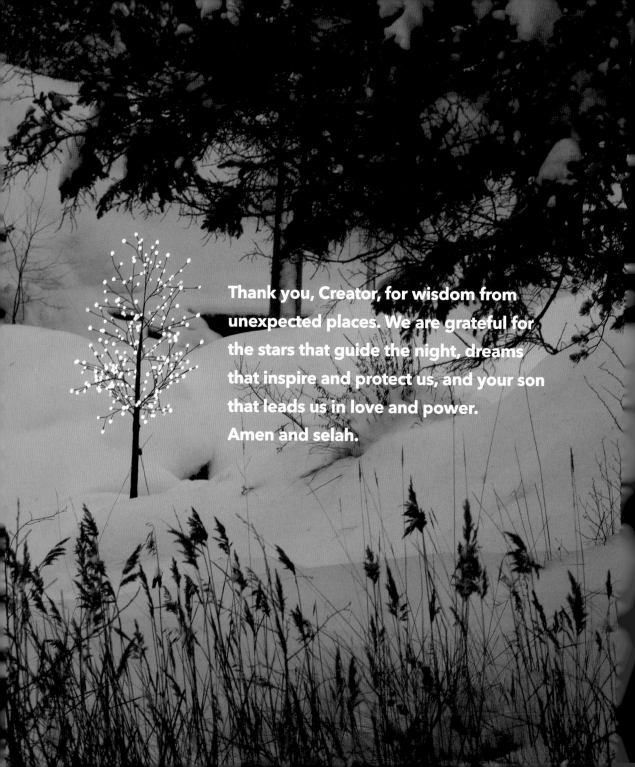

Thank you, Creator, for wisdom from unexpected places. We are grateful for the stars that guide the night, dreams that inspire and protect us, and your son that leads us in love and power.
Amen and selah.

Vince Amlin is Co-Pastor of Bethany United Church of Christ in Chicago and co-planter of Gilead Chicago.

Talitha Arnold is Senior Minister of the United Church of Santa Fe (UCC) in New Mexico. She is the author of Mark (Parts 1 and 2) in the Listen Up! Bible study series.

Quinn G. Caldwell is a father, husband, homesteader, and preacher living in rural upstate New York. He is the author of *All I Really Want: Readings for a Modern Christmas.*

Lillian Daniel is Senior Pastor at First Congregational Church in Dubuque, Iowa. She is the author of *Tired of Apologizing for a Church I Don't Belong To* among other titles.

Kaji Dou\u0161a is Senior Minister of The Park Avenue Christian Church in New York City.

John Edgerton is Lead Pastor at First United Church of Oak Park, Illinois.

Rachel Hackenberg serves on the national staff for the United Church of Christ. She is the author of the popular Lenten book, *Writing to God*, among other titles.

Ann Kansfield is Co-Pastor of the Greenpoint Reformed Church in Brooklyn (UCC/RCA) and Chaplain for the Fire Department of the City of New York.

Vicki Kemper is Pastor of First Church Amherst (UCC) in Amherst, Massachusetts.

Matt Laney is a United Church of Christ minister and the author of *Pride Wars,* a fantasy series for young readers.

Phiwa Langeni is Founder/Director of Salus Center and Pastor of Salus Center UCC and First Congregational UCC-Ypsilanti. They are a parent, speaker, writer, transitional coach, designer, and low-key fashion head.

Mary Luti is a long-time seminary educator and the author of *Teresa of Avila's Way* and numerous articles on the practice of the Christian life.

Chris Mereschuk is an Unsettled Pastor in the Southern New England Conference with a call to transitional ministry.

Liz Miller serves as the pastor of Edgewood United Church (UCC) in East Lansing, Michigan.

Marilyn Pagán-Banks serves as Pastor of San Lucas UCC, Executive Director of A Just Harvest, and Adjunct Professor at McCormick Theological Seminary in Chicago.

Kenneth L. Samuel is Pastor of Victory for the World Church (UCC) in Stone Mountain, Georgia. He is the author of *Solomon's Success: Four Essential Keys to Leadership*.

Donna Schaper is Pastor at the Orient Congregational Church on the far end of Long Island, New York. Her newest book is *Remove the Pews: Spiritual Possibilities for Sacred Spaces*.

Martha Spong is a UCC pastor, clergy coach, and editor of *The Words of Her Mouth: Psalms for the Struggle*.

Naomi Washington-Leapheart is the Director for Faith-Based and Interfaith Affairs for the Mayor's Office of Public Engagement in Philadelphia, PA.